Psychology
Positive

Alexa Murphy

Copyright Page

Index

Introduction to Positive Psychology

Positive psychology is an approach within psychology that seeks to understand and foster the best in us. Unlike other branches of psychology that focus primarily on problems, mental illness or distress, positive psychology focuses on positive emotions, well-being, personal strengths and the ability we have to be happy and lead a fulfilling life. Its aim is to help us improve the quality of our lives by teaching us to develop a more optimistic and resilient mindset.

This approach is born out of the need to balance the study of the mind. For many years, psychologists have devoted themselves to studying what makes us suffer, to understanding mental disorders, and to finding solutions to alleviate emotional pain. While all of this is important, it is not enough. Positive psychology invites us to ask ourselves: why not also study what makes us happy? Why not look for the keys to a satisfying and fulfilling life? This field is based on the idea that we all have the potential to live better, but to achieve this, we need to learn to train our minds to focus on the positive.

One of the first things we need to understand about positive psychology is that it is not about ignoring problems or pretending that everything in life is perfect. We all face difficulties and difficult moments, but what this approach proposes is to learn to see those challenges from a different perspective. Instead of getting stuck in the problem, positive psychology teaches us to focus on our strengths, on the solutions, and on the opportunities that each obstacle can offer us to grow. In this way, little by little, we transform our mentality.

Imagine for a moment that your mind is like a garden. If you don't take care of it, weeds start to grow and, without you realizing it, they take over the space, suffocating the flowers and plants that you really want to see bloom. Positive psychology teaches you to be the gardener of your own mind, to recognize those weeds that represent negative thoughts and replace them with flowers, that is, with positive and constructive thoughts. Over time, that garden becomes a healthier and more beautiful space.

One of the most important tools in positive psychology is optimism. Being optimistic doesn't mean ignoring reality or believing that everything will be perfect, but rather having the confidence that even when things get tough, you can find a solution or a way to get through. It's seeing the glass as half full instead of half empty. For example, if you lose a job, instead of falling into despair, you can think about the opportunity that is presented to you to look for something better or even start a project of your own. This type of thinking not only makes us feel better emotionally, but it also gives us the strength to make better decisions and face problems with a more constructive attitude.

Another key aspect of positive psychology is gratitude. Sometimes, we focus so much on what we lack that we forget all the good things we already have. Practicing gratitude helps us remember that even though not everything in life is perfect, there is always something we can be grateful for. It can be something as simple as a beautiful sunrise, a meal you enjoyed, or the company of a friend. The simple act of stopping to appreciate these small moments helps us reprogram our minds to focus on the positive, rather than getting caught up in the negative.

Emotional well-being is also closely related to a sense of purpose. Positive psychology teaches us that when we feel that our actions have purpose or meaning, our lives become more fulfilling. Finding that purpose is not always easy, but it can be anything that makes us feel fulfilled, from helping others to pursuing a personal goal or developing a skill. The important thing is that by having a clear direction in life, our positive emotions increase and our mind becomes stronger in the face of adversity.

It's important to note that positive psychology isn't something that works overnight. Changing our mindset takes practice, effort, and consistency. But the good news is that over time, those small changes in how we view the world add up and have a big impact on our daily lives. Just like any skill, we can train our minds to be more positive, more resilient, and better able to face life's challenges with an optimistic attitude.

In short, positive psychology offers us a new way of looking at life. It reminds us that although we all face difficulties, we also have the power to decide how to respond to those difficulties. It teaches us to cultivate optimism, gratitude and a sense of purpose, which are essential tools for leading a happier and more fulfilling life. Most importantly, it reminds us that it is not about being perfect or avoiding problems, but about learning to face them with a positive and constructive mindset. This is the key to a healthier and more fulfilling life.

Reprogramming the Mind towards Positive Thinking

Reprogramming our minds towards positive thinking is a process that allows us to change the way we interpret the world and how we react to what happens to us. We have all, to a greater or lesser extent, developed thought patterns throughout our lives. These patterns are like paths that our mind travels over and over again. If those paths are full of negative thoughts, such as pessimism, constant criticism or fear, our way of seeing the world will be affected by it. But the good news is that, just like a muscle, we can train our minds to change those patterns and focus on the positive.

The first step to reprogramming our minds is to recognize negative thoughts when they appear. Often, these thoughts go unnoticed because we are so used to them that we accept them as normal. For example, you might be working on a project and if something goes wrong, your first reaction might be to think that you are not good enough or that you always fail. This type of negative thinking is automatic, but it is not real. Simply being aware of these thoughts is the first step to changing them.

Once we identify negative thoughts, the next step is to challenge them. This means asking ourselves if those thoughts are truly true or if we are exaggerating the situation. Many times, our mind tricks us into believing that something is worse than it really is. If, for example, you think that you will never succeed in a certain area, you can stop for a moment and remember all the times you have achieved something. Challenging negative thoughts does not mean ignoring reality, but rather seeing it from a more balanced perspective.

Another very useful strategy to reprogram your mind is to change your focus. Instead of thinking about what could go wrong, we can focus on what can go right. For example, if you have a job interview and you are nervous, instead of imagining all the ways you could fail, try visualizing yourself answering the questions with confidence and showing off your skills. This simple shift in focus can transform how you feel and how you mentally prepare for the situation.

Positive affirmations are another powerful tool in the mental reprogramming process. Affirmations are simple phrases that we repeat to ourselves to reinforce a positive thought. For example, if you feel insecure before a presentation, you could repeat phrases like "I am capable," "I have everything it takes to do well," or "I am confident in my abilities." By repeating these affirmations, you are training your mind to believe in them. It may feel a little artificial at first, but over time, these affirmations start to become part of your belief system and replace negative thoughts.

A key point in this process is consistency. It is not enough to practice positive thinking once in a while. Just as we cannot strengthen our muscles by going to the gym just once, we cannot change our way of thinking with a single effort. We need to practice daily. The good news is that the more you do it, the easier it will become. Little by little, the negative mental pathways will weaken and the positive ones will become stronger.

In addition to affirmations and changing our focus, there is something else we can do: surround ourselves with positivity. Our environment has a huge impact on our way of thinking. If we spend a lot of time with negative people or in toxic environments, it will be harder to maintain a positive mindset. On the contrary, if we surround ourselves with people who support us, who encourage us and who have an optimistic outlook on life, it will be easier to reprogram our mind. This does not mean that we should avoid people who are going through a bad time at all costs, but we should make sure that we balance our environment so that it is not all negative.

Gratitude also plays a key role in this process. When we practice gratitude, we are training ourselves to see the positive in our lives, even in difficult times. A very simple exercise you can do every day is to take a few minutes at the end of the day to write down three things you are grateful for. These can be big things, like the support of your family, or small things, like having enjoyed a good meal. This exercise helps shift your focus and teaches you to see the good even in the most difficult days.

One of the biggest obstacles we face when trying to reprogram our minds is self-criticism. Often, we are our own worst critics. We judge ourselves harshly when we make mistakes or when we don't meet our expectations. This constant self-criticism keeps us stuck in a cycle of negative thinking. To break this cycle, it's important to practice self-compassion. This means treating ourselves with the same kindness and understanding we would offer a friend. If we make a mistake, instead of mentally punishing ourselves, we can remind ourselves that everyone makes mistakes and that they don't define us. Self-compassion allows us to be kinder to ourselves and helps us maintain a positive mindset even during difficult times.

Another important aspect of mental reprogramming is stress management. When we are under a lot of stress, our mind tends to automatically turn negative. We worry about the future, about what may go wrong, or we feel overwhelmed by responsibilities. In order to reprogram our mind, it is essential to learn how to manage stress effectively. This can involve techniques such as meditation, deep breathing, or simply taking a break when needed. By reducing stress, it is easier to maintain a positive focus and not fall into negative thought patterns.

In short, reprogramming our minds toward positive thinking is not an immediate process, but it is entirely possible. It takes time, effort, and consistent practice, but the benefits are enormous. By learning to identify and challenge negative thoughts, by practicing positive affirmations, by surrounding ourselves with optimistic influences, and by managing stress, we can change the way we think. And when we change the way we think, we change our lives.

Alexa Murphy

The Power of Optimism

Optimism is one of the most powerful tools we can have in life. It's not just about smiling all the time or pretending that everything is fine when it isn't. Optimism goes way beyond that. It's a way of seeing the world and facing it that gives us the strength to keep going, even when things don't go the way we expect. Having an optimistic mindset means believing that even when difficulties arise, we are capable of overcoming them and that there is always a solution, an opportunity or a lesson to be learned in every situation.

To understand the true power of optimism, it is important to know that our thoughts directly affect how we feel and, ultimately, how we act. If we constantly think that things will go wrong, we are likely to feel anxious, frustrated or unmotivated, which also affects our actions. On the other hand, if we think that things can go well, our emotions change: we feel calmer, motivated and more confident to face any challenge. This change in our thoughts and emotions leads us to make better decisions and act more effectively.

Optimism is not about denying reality or pretending that everything is perfect. Optimistic people are not immune to problems, but the difference is that they have a way of looking at those problems that helps them handle them better. Instead of focusing on what is wrong, they look for solutions. Instead of giving up in the face of difficulties, they ask themselves: what can I learn from this? How can I improve the situation? This mindset not only helps reduce stress, but also increases the likelihood of finding a positive way out of problems.

Imagine you have to cross a bridge, but from where you're standing, the bridge looks long, unstable, and with lots of obstacles in the way. If you focus only on how difficult it is, you'll probably feel overwhelmed and maybe decide not to cross it. But if you instead think about what's on the other side of the bridge, the opportunity that awaits you, and the ways you can overcome those obstacles, you'll feel more motivated to try. That's the difference optimism makes: it gives you the energy and drive to keep going, even when the path isn't easy.

Optimism also has a direct impact on our health. Numerous studies have shown that people who have an optimistic attitude tend to live longer and enjoy better physical and mental health. This is because optimism reduces stress and anxiety levels, which has a positive effect on the immune system and the heart. In addition, optimistic people tend to take better care of themselves, as they are more motivated to exercise, eat well, and look for ways to maintain a healthy lifestyle.

Optimism also improves our relationships with others. When we are optimistic, we not only feel better about ourselves, but we also project that energy toward others. People are often drawn to those who have a positive attitude, as being around someone who is optimistic can be contagious. Optimism creates an environment of support and collaboration, which strengthens personal and professional relationships. Additionally, when we face problems in our relationships, an optimistic mindset allows us to view those problems as opportunities to grow and improve, rather than seeing them as the end of the relationship.

Another important aspect of optimism is that it helps us handle failure better. We have all experienced failure at some point. Whether it is at work, in our personal goals, or in our relationships, failure is inevitable. However, what really matters is not the failure itself, but how we interpret it. A pessimistic person may see failure as a sign that they are not good enough or that they will never succeed. But an optimistic person sees failure as a lesson, as an opportunity to learn something new and improve. Optimism gives us the ability to get up after every fall, to keep going, and to keep trying, even when things don't go as planned.

A good example of how optimism can change our lives is to think about sports. Athletes who have an optimistic mindset tend to perform better than those who don't. This is because they believe in their ability to improve and in their ability to overcome the challenges they face. Even when they lose, optimistic athletes don't give up; instead, they focus on how they can improve for next time. This mindset is applicable to any area of our lives. When we believe that we can improve, that we can overcome obstacles, and that we can achieve our goals, we are more inclined to put in the effort necessary to do so.

Optimism is also related to perseverance. Optimistic people tend to be more persistent because they believe that their efforts will eventually pay off. They are not easily discouraged by setbacks and are willing to keep trying until they achieve what they set out to do. On the other hand, people who have a negative or pessimistic outlook tend to give up faster because they believe that success is not possible for them. This is where optimism makes a big difference: it gives us the strength to keep going, even when things get tough.

It is important to note that optimism is not something we are either born with or not. It is not a fixed characteristic that some people have and others don't. Optimism is something that can be developed over time. We can train our minds to be more optimistic, to see the good in every situation, and to face problems with a positive attitude. Like any habit, it takes practice, but the results are worth it.

In short, the power of optimism lies in its ability to transform our lives. It helps us feel better, act more confidently, improve our relationships, and overcome challenges more easily. Optimism doesn't eliminate problems, but it gives us the tools to face them with a healthier and more constructive attitude. Most importantly, it reminds us that even though the road may not always be easy, there is always a light at the end of the tunnel if we are willing to look for it.

The Impact of Positive Thinking on Health

Positive thinking not only influences how we feel emotionally, but it also has a direct impact on our physical health. The relationship between mind and body is stronger than we might imagine, and studies have shown that the way we think affects our health in profound ways. Having a positive attitude is not only a benefit to our mood, but it can help us live longer, enjoy a better quality of life, and stay healthier overall.

When we talk about positive thinking, we are referring to the tendency to focus on the good that happens in our lives, rather than getting caught up in the negative. People who practice positive thinking tend to see challenges as opportunities, are confident that they can overcome difficulties, and focus on solutions rather than problems. This, in turn, reduces stress, one of the biggest enemies of our health.

Chronic stress is one of the main causes of many health problems, such as high blood pressure, heart disease, diabetes, and a weakened immune system. When we are constantly stressed, our body releases hormones such as cortisol, which, in excess, can damage our organs and systems. However, positive thinking acts as a natural antidote to stress. When we adopt an optimistic attitude and focus on the positive, our stress levels decrease, which has a direct impact on our physical health.

In addition to stress, positive thinking also helps to improve our immune system. Our immune system is our body's natural defense against illness and viruses. Research has shown that people who maintain a positive attitude tend to have a stronger immune system, which means they are less likely to get sick, and when they do, they usually recover faster. This is because the body and mind are deeply connected, and when our mind is in a positive state, our physical defenses are strengthened.

Another important aspect of the impact of positive thinking on health is the reduction of the risk of heart disease. People who practice positive thinking tend to have fewer heart problems, and if they do develop a disease, they tend to handle it better than those who have a more negative attitude. This may be because positive thoughts help maintain lower blood pressure and reduce inflammation in the body, key factors in preventing heart disease.

Plus, positive thinking also motivates us to adopt healthier habits. When we have an optimistic mindset, we are more likely to take care of our bodies. People who practice positive thinking are often more willing to exercise, maintain a balanced diet, and avoid harmful behaviors like smoking or excessive drinking. This is no coincidence, as when we think positively, we believe that our well-being matters, and that drives us to make choices that favor our health.

Physical exercise, for example, is an activity that has a very positive impact on our physical and mental health. People who adopt a positive attitude tend to see exercise not as a burden or an obligation, but as a way to feel better, release tension and take care of their body. When we think positively about exercise, it is easier to maintain a consistent routine, which contributes to improving our cardiovascular health, strengthening our muscles and improving our mood.

Positive thinking also helps us sleep better. Sleep is essential for our health, as during the night, our body recovers and repairs damage sustained during the day. However, when our mind is filled with worries and negative thoughts, we may have trouble falling asleep or sleeping soundly. People who practice positive thinking tend to have less difficulty relaxing before bed, allowing them to rest better and wake up with more energy the next day. Sleeping well not only makes us feel better, but it also helps improve our immune system, our memory, and our ability to concentrate.

Positive thinking also has a protective effect against the effects of aging. People who maintain an optimistic attitude throughout their lives tend to age more healthily, both physically and mentally. Research has shown that those who view aging as a natural and positive part of life, rather than fearing it or viewing it as something negative, tend to maintain better cognitive and physical abilities in old age. In addition, positive thinking is linked to greater longevity. Optimistic people tend to live longer than those who are more pessimistic, in part due to the beneficial effects that optimism has on overall health.

Another impact of positive thinking on health is its ability to help us better cope with serious illnesses. People who adopt a positive attitude when facing an illness often have better recovery outcomes. This doesn't mean that positive thinking cures illnesses, but it can help us cope with the healing process with more mental and emotional strength. Patients who maintain an optimistic mindset tend to follow their treatments better, maintain better communication with their doctors, and face medical challenges with more hope, which can make a big difference in their recovery.

The impact of positive thinking on mental health is also significant. When we practice positive thinking, our mind becomes more resilient in the face of challenges. People who think positively tend to experience less depression, anxiety, and other mental disorders. This is because optimism helps us see difficulties as temporary and manageable, rather than feeling overwhelmed by them. Additionally, positive thinking allows us to build higher self-esteem, which helps us feel more confident and capable of facing any challenge.

It's important to understand that positive thinking doesn't mean ignoring life's problems or difficulties. We all face difficult times, and it's normal to feel sad or worried sometimes. But positive thinking teaches us not to get caught up in those negative emotions, but to find a way to move forward. It allows us to see the light at the end of the tunnel, even in the darkest moments, and gives us the strength to keep fighting for our health and well-being.

In short, the impact of positive thinking on health is enormous. Not only does it help us feel better emotionally, but it also has tangible physical benefits, such as reduced stress, improved immune system, prevention of heart disease, and increased longevity. Plus, it motivates us to take care of our bodies, sleep better, and face illness with more mental strength. Practicing positive thinking is one of the best things we can do for our health, and while it may take effort and practice, the long-term benefits are worth every minute of that effort.

Gratitude as a Key to Mental Success

Gratitude is one of the most powerful tools we have at our disposal to improve our mental and emotional health. Often, when we think of success, we associate it with external accomplishments: achieving goals, having a successful career, or accomplishing certain objectives. However, true success—the kind that brings us peace of mind and lasting happiness—has a lot to do with how we feel inside. And gratitude is the key to achieving that kind of success.

Practicing gratitude means taking a moment to acknowledge and appreciate all the good we already have in our lives. It's not about ignoring problems or pretending everything is perfect, but rather learning to focus on the positive, rather than focusing only on what we lack or what isn't going the way we want. It's often easy to fall into the trap of focusing on the negative: on mistakes, difficulties, or what we think we're missing. But when we practice gratitude, we change that focus and begin to see the world through different eyes.

Gratitude has a direct impact on our mind. When we are grateful, we activate a part of our brain that makes us feel good, generating positive emotions such as happiness, satisfaction, and peace. This happens because gratitude makes us realize that, despite the problems we may be facing, there are many things to be grateful for. This simple shift in our perspective helps us reduce stress, feel calmer, and improve our overall mental health.

A simple example of how gratitude can transform our mindset is when we are faced with a challenge. Instead of focusing on how difficult the situation is or the fear of failure, we can give thanks for the opportunity to learn something new or to get better at what we do. This practice completely changes the way we approach problems, as instead of seeing them as insurmountable obstacles, we see them as opportunities to grow.

Gratitude also helps us to have a more realistic view of our lives. Often, when we don't practice gratitude, we tend to underestimate what we already have. It's easy to take for granted things as simple as health, family, work, or even the possibility of enjoying a new day. However, when we start to be aware of all these things and to be grateful for them, we realize how lucky we are, and that gives us a feeling of fulfillment and success that doesn't depend on external circumstances.

Another important aspect of gratitude is that it allows us to enjoy the present more. Often, we spend our lives worrying about the future or regretting the past, which prevents us from enjoying what is happening in the moment. However, when we are grateful, we learn to appreciate the here and now. Sometimes, we just need to stop for a moment to notice the little things around us: a sunrise, a conversation with a friend, a meal we enjoyed. By being grateful for these moments, our lives become more meaningful, and we feel more connected to ourselves and the world.

Practicing gratitude also has benefits for our relationships. When we are grateful, we tend to see the best in the people around us. Instead of focusing on their flaws or what annoys us about them, we begin to appreciate their qualities, their kind gestures, and their company. This shift in perspective strengthens our relationships, as we become more understanding, more patient, and more caring. Furthermore, when we express our gratitude to others, whether through words or actions, we create an environment of trust and caring that improves the quality of our interactions.

It's important to note that gratitude isn't something that comes automatically. Often, we have to make a conscious effort to practice it. Life can be complicated, and sometimes it's hard to see the silver lining when we're dealing with problems. However, gratitude is like a muscle: the more we practice it, the stronger it becomes. A simple exercise that can help us cultivate gratitude is to keep a gratitude journal. Each day, we can take a few minutes to write down three things we're grateful for. It doesn't matter how big or small they are; the important thing is to recognize and appreciate them.

Over time, this habit will help us shift our mindset and become more aware of all the good things we have.

Gratitude also protects us against the negative effects of comparisons. In today's world, it's all too easy to fall into the temptation of comparing ourselves to others, especially with social media constantly showing us other people's seemingly perfect lives. However, when we practice gratitude, we stop focusing on what others have or do, and start appreciating what we already have in our own lives. This frees us from the need to compare ourselves and allows us to feel more content and satisfied with who we are and what we've accomplished.

Gratitude also gives us a broader perspective on life. It reminds us that we are not alone, that there are many people who have contributed to our well-being in one way or another. Whether it is family who supports us, friends who encourage us, or even strangers who, with a small gesture, have made our day better, gratitude connects us to others. This connection gives us a sense of belonging and purpose, which contributes to our mental and emotional success.

In short, gratitude is one of the most important keys to achieving mental success. Not only does it improve our mental and emotional health, but it also helps us enjoy life more, strengthen our relationships, and have a more positive outlook on ourselves and the world. Practicing gratitude doesn't mean that everything will be perfect or that we won't face challenges, but it does give us the tools to face those challenges with a more positive and constructive mindset. Most importantly, it teaches us to value what we already have, which gives us a sense of success and satisfaction that goes beyond any material achievement.

Focus on Solutions, Not Problems

In life, we all face problems. It's part of the human experience. From small setbacks to bigger challenges, problems will always be there, and we can't avoid them entirely. However, what really defines our success and well-being is not the number of problems we have, but how we choose to deal with them. One of the most valuable lessons we can learn is to focus on solutions, not problems. This simple shift in focus can transform the way we live and help us overcome any difficulty with a more positive and effective mindset.

When we encounter a problem, it's natural to feel frustrated, worried, or even overwhelmed. Sometimes, we get caught up thinking over and over how bad the problem is, how it affects us, and all the things that could go wrong. This type of thinking, while common, doesn't get us anywhere. The more we focus on the problem, the bigger and more complicated it seems. It's like we're looking through a magnifying glass: every negative detail is magnified, and it becomes harder and harder for us to see a way out.

But here's the key: Problems, in and of themselves, aren't what really cause us stress or distress. What really affects us is our reaction to them. If we spend all our time worrying about the problem, we're just adding more stress to the situation. If we shift our focus to solutions, however, we begin to take control of the situation. Suddenly, what seemed impossible to solve becomes a challenge we can manage.

Focusing on solutions means first accepting that problems exist, but not letting them dominate us. Instead of getting stuck in "Why is this happening to me?" or "This is too hard," we should ask ourselves, "What can I do to fix this?" This shift in question is powerful, because it takes us from a position of victim to a position of power. We are no longer at the mercy of the problem, but become the protagonists of our own story, making active choices to improve our situation.

One of the reasons why many people feel paralyzed by problems is because they believe they need to find a perfect or definitive solution. But the reality is that, in most cases, there is no single perfect solution. What matters is to start moving in the right direction, taking small steps that bring us closer to the solution. Maybe the first step will not solve the problem completely, but it will give us the necessary momentum to continue moving forward and, over time, find the most appropriate solution.

Another important part of focusing on solutions is learning to view problems as opportunities for growth. It may sound cliché, but it's true: every challenge we face gives us the chance to learn something new, develop skills we didn't have before, and become emotionally stronger. For example, if you have a problem at work, instead of thinking about how it's negatively affecting you, you might view it as an opportunity to improve your conflict-resolution skills or develop new strategies that will make you more efficient in the future. This shift in perspective not only reduces stress, but it also motivates you to face the problem with a more positive attitude.

Additionally, when we focus on solutions, we become more creative. Instead of getting stuck in a fixed mindset, we start thinking outside the box. We look for alternatives, consider different approaches, and are more willing to try new things. Sometimes the solution to a problem isn't obvious at first, but if we keep an open mind and keep looking, we can find solutions we would never have imagined if we had stayed focused on just the problem.

Another important aspect of focusing on solutions is that it helps us maintain a progress mindset. As we begin to take actions to solve a problem, even if they are small, we feel like we are moving forward. This gives us a sense of accomplishment and motivates us to keep going. In contrast, when we only focus on the problem, we feel like we are stuck, which can lead to frustration and, in some cases, even hopelessness. But each small step toward a solution is a reminder that we are doing something to improve the situation, and that gives us the energy to continue.

It's also important to remember that we don't always need to solve problems alone. Sometimes the best way to find a solution is to ask for help. It may be that someone else has already faced a similar problem and has ideas or experiences that can help us. Or maybe we simply need a new perspective to see the situation from a different angle. Asking for help is not a sign of weakness, but of wisdom. It allows us to access resources we wouldn't otherwise have and helps us solve problems more quickly and effectively.

Furthermore, focusing on solutions doesn't mean ignoring the negatives or being naive about problems. It's important to acknowledge challenges and be realistic about the difficulties we face. But rather than getting caught up in the negative, we use that awareness as a basis for finding solutions. This approach allows us to be proactive rather than reactive. We're not denying the reality of the problem, we're simply choosing not to let it consume us.

Another important point is that when we focus on solutions, we are cultivating an abundance mindset. This means that instead of seeing difficulties as insurmountable limitations, we begin to see the world as full of possibilities. We believe that there is always a solution, a way out, a way to make things better. This mindset empowers us, as it makes us feel that we have the internal and external resources to face any challenge that comes our way.

In short, focusing on solutions, rather than problems, is one of the most important skills we can develop to lead a more positive and successful life. It allows us to take control of our circumstances, be proactive and creative, and move towards our goals with confidence and determination. Problems will always be there, but how we deal with them is entirely up to us. By shifting our focus to solutions, we not only solve problems more effectively, but we also become more resilient, optimistic, and capable people. This approach allows us to live with less stress and a greater sense of accomplishment and satisfaction. And best of all, with practice, we can all learn to focus on solutions and transform the way we view and deal with life's challenges.

Facing Challenges with a Positive Mindset

Facing life's challenges with a positive mindset can make the difference between feeling defeated by difficulties or turning them into opportunities for personal growth. Throughout our lives, we all face challenging moments: unexpected situations, seemingly insurmountable obstacles, or difficult decisions. These challenges can arise in any area, whether at work, in our personal relationships, in our health, or even in our own thoughts and emotions. However, what really defines the outcome of these experiences is not so much the challenge itself, but how we choose to face it.

A positive mindset doesn't mean that we ignore problems or pretend that everything is perfect when it isn't. Being positive is not synonymous with being naive or denying reality. On the contrary, having a positive mindset involves accepting reality, but choosing how to react to it. When we adopt a positive mindset in the face of challenges, we are choosing to look beyond the immediate problem. We are choosing to look for solutions, learn from the situation, and maintain the hope that, with effort and patience, things can improve.

One of the first steps to approaching a challenge with a positive mindset is to change the way we view it. Often, when we encounter an obstacle, our first reaction is to think about the negative: how it affects us, everything that could go wrong, or how unfair the situation seems. These types of thoughts only sink us deeper into worry and stress. However, if we change our perspective and start seeing challenges as opportunities, we open ourselves up to a world of possibilities. Every challenge, no matter how difficult, can teach us something valuable. It can help us develop new skills, discover strengths we didn't know we had, or grow in ways we never imagined.

For example, imagine you're facing a challenge at work. Maybe you have a tight deadline, or you've been assigned a task you've never done before. It's easy to feel overwhelmed in situations like this and start to doubt your abilities. But instead of focusing on how difficult the challenge is, you could ask yourself, "What can I learn from this? How can I improve my skills or my organization to best meet this challenge?" This simple shift in focus helps us feel more in control and view the challenge as an opportunity for growth, rather than something that is beyond us.

Another important aspect of a positive mindset is patience. Facing challenges is not always easy, and many times the results are not seen immediately. It is natural to want things to be resolved quickly and perfectly, but the reality is that some challenges require time and effort to be overcome. Maintaining a positive mindset means being patient with ourselves and with the process. Accepting that there will be times when things will not go as we expect, but that does not mean that we cannot continue moving forward. Every step we take, no matter how small, brings us closer to overcoming the challenge, and maintaining that patience is key to not giving up along the way.

Additionally, a positive mindset allows us to stay calm in the midst of the storm. When we face a challenge, it's easy to let negative emotions like fear, frustration, or anxiety take over. But when we adopt a positive attitude, we give ourselves the space to breathe, to reflect, and to make clearer decisions. Staying calm doesn't mean we don't feel pressure or worry, but it does mean we don't let those emotions take control of our actions. We give ourselves permission to feel, but also to act from a place of serenity and confidence that we can find a solution.

A key part of facing challenges with a positive mindset is believing in our own abilities. Often times when we face an obstacle, we start to doubt ourselves. We think we're not good enough, that we don't have what it takes to overcome the situation, or that it's too difficult for us. But the truth is that we all have within us the ability to face any challenge, even if it doesn't seem like it at the moment. The key is to trust ourselves, our skills, and our ability to learn and adapt. Even if we don't know how to solve a problem right away, we have the ability to look for solutions, ask for help if necessary, and keep trying until we find a way.

Perseverance is another essential component of a positive mindset. Sometimes, challenges aren't solved in one attempt. We may have to try different approaches, make mistakes along the way, or face temporary failures. But a positive mindset helps us see each obstacle as part of the process, not as an end point. It allows us to keep going, even when things don't go our way. Perseverance is what keeps us moving, what pushes us to keep looking for solutions, and what ultimately leads us to overcome any challenge.

It's also important to remember that we're not alone in our struggle. Facing challenges with a positive mindset doesn't mean we have to do everything on our own. Sometimes, asking for help or support is the best way to deal with a difficult situation. Surrounding ourselves with people who encourage us, give us a different perspective, or simply listen to us can make a big difference. Plus, sharing our challenges with others can ease some of the emotional burden and remind us that we're not alone in our troubles.

Facing challenges with a positive mindset also has an impact on our mental and physical health. The stress we experience when facing a problem can affect our energy, our sleep, and our overall well-being. But when we adopt a positive attitude, we are reducing that stress. We are taking control of our situation instead of letting the problem control us. This shift in focus allows us to face challenges with a clearer mind and a greater sense of well-being.

Finally, a positive mindset allows us to see beyond the immediate challenge. It helps us keep perspective that although a challenge may seem huge at the moment, it is only a part of our life, not the whole. Sometimes when we are in the midst of a difficult situation, it seems like everything revolves around that problem, but a positive mindset reminds us that there are many other things in our lives to be grateful for and that, in time, this challenge will pass, too.

In conclusion, facing challenges with a positive mindset is a skill that we can all develop. It requires effort, but the benefits are enormous. It allows us to face problems with more serenity, confidence and perseverance. It helps us learn from our experiences, grow and maintain a broader perspective on life. Although challenges will always be present, a positive mindset gives us the tools to overcome them and come out stronger on the other side.

The Importance of Surrounding Yourself with Positive Influences

Surrounding ourselves with positive influences is one of the most important decisions we can make for our emotional, mental, and even physical well-being. The people we spend time with, the places we frequent, the activities we engage in, and the messages we receive from the outside world have a huge impact on the way we think, our emotions, and ultimately the quality of our lives. Although we may not notice it right away, the influences around us have the power to shape the way we view the world and how we respond to the situations we face. That's why choosing our influences carefully is critical to maintaining a positive mindset.

First, it is important to understand what influences are exactly. In this context, we are talking about everything around us that, in some way, has an effect on us. These can be people, such as our friends, family, coworkers, or even public figures that we follow on social media. They can also be the places where we spend time, such as our work environment, home, or spaces where we socialize. Also, we should not forget the media, the music we listen to, the books we read, the movies we watch, and everything we consume in terms of information. Each of these elements has the potential to influence how we think and feel.

One of the most powerful reasons to surround ourselves with positive influences is that, as human beings, we are incredibly susceptible to what happens around us. Our emotions and thoughts are like sponges that absorb what we see, hear, and experience in our daily lives. If we spend a lot of time surrounded by negativity, constant criticism, or people who demotivate us, it is likely that this negative energy will also be reflected in our own attitude. For example, if we constantly hear pessimistic comments about the future or destructive criticism about our capabilities, we will begin to doubt our own abilities and feel less capable of achieving our goals.

On the other hand, when we surround ourselves with people and environments that encourage growth, positivity, and mutual support, our mindset changes as well. We begin to see the world from a more optimistic perspective. We feel more inspired to improve, to look for solutions instead of getting stuck in problems, and to believe in our potential to overcome challenges. Positive influences act as a constant reminder that hardships are temporary and that there is always a way to move forward, even in the most difficult times.

The people we spend our time with play a crucial role in this process. Think about it for a moment: If you spend most of your time with someone who always complains, who never sees the bright side of things, or who constantly criticizes others, chances are you'll end up adopting some of those attitudes without realizing it. You might even start feeling more emotionally exhausted after interacting with that person. This happens because negativity is contagious. Just as we can absorb positivity from those around us, we can also absorb negativity.

That's why it's essential to choose the people you spend time with carefully. It's not about abandoning everyone who is going through a bad time or who has a negative attitude from time to time. We're all human and we go through ups and downs. But it is important to surround ourselves with people who support us, inspire us, and motivate us to be the best version of ourselves. Look for people who make you feel good about yourself, who encourage you to follow your dreams, and who see the positive side of life. These people will not only make your day-to-day life more enjoyable, but they will also help you maintain a positive mindset in the face of challenges.

In addition to people, the physical environment we find ourselves in also has an impact on our mindset. Imagine you work in a messy, dark, and noisy place. You are likely to feel more stressed or unmotivated, simply by being in that environment. On the contrary, if you work in a clean, well-lit, and quiet space, you will feel more at peace and more energized to tackle your tasks. This applies to all aspects of our lives: the places we spend time in, whether at work, at home, or in our leisure activities, can directly affect our mental state.

That's why it's helpful to make small changes to our environment to ensure that they support a positive mindset. It can be something as simple as organizing your desk, decorating your space with objects that inspire you, or spending more time outdoors. The environment you create around you can be a reflection of your mental state, and at the same time, it can influence it. The more positive, organized, and pleasant your surroundings are, the easier it will be to maintain an optimistic and productive attitude.

Additionally, it's important to be mindful of the type of content we consume. Nowadays, we are constantly exposed to an onslaught of information, especially through social media, television, and digital media. We are not always aware of how all that content affects our way of thinking. If we spend hours watching negative news or comparing ourselves to unrealistic images of success on social media, we are likely to start feeling discouraged or insecure. But if, on the other hand, we choose to consume content that inspires us, teaches us something new, or makes us feel good, that impact will be much more positive in our daily lives.

Take, for example, the decision to read books that motivate us or listen to podcasts that help us develop a stronger, more optimistic mindset. These types of influences provide us with tools and perspectives that we can apply in our daily lives. They remind us that success and happiness are not always immediate, but that with effort and a positive attitude, we can achieve our goals. The content we consume acts as a mirror for our thoughts and emotions, and if we consciously choose to consume positive influences, that reflection will be much more beneficial to our well-being.

One aspect that is also key to the impact of positive influences is how they help us stay focused on what really matters. Often, we get distracted by the worries or negative comments of others, which can divert our attention from our goals and desires. But when we surround ourselves with positive influences, it is easier to stay focused on what is important to us. These influences act as constant reminders to keep going, despite the difficulties, and encourage us not to lose sight of our goals.

Finally, surrounding ourselves with positive influences not only improves our own mindset, but it also helps us to be a positive influence for others. When we are in a good mental state, when we feel supported and motivated, it is easier to transmit that positive energy to the people around us. We become a beacon of optimism for others, which in turn can help them face their own challenges with a more positive attitude. In this way, by choosing to surround ourselves with positive influences, we are not only improving our own lives, but also contributing to the well-being of others.

In short, the importance of surrounding ourselves with positive influences cannot be understated. From the people we interact with to the environment we create and the content we consume, each of these factors has a significant impact on our mindset and how we deal with life's challenges. By making conscious choices to surround ourselves with positivity, we are creating a space conducive to growth, happiness and success. Not only does this help us maintain a stronger, more optimistic mindset, but it also allows us to be a positive influence for others.

Programming Your Mind for Success

Programming our mind for success is one of the most powerful steps we can take in life. Everything we do, how we think, the decisions we make, and the way we face challenges are directly influenced by our mindset. If our mind is aligned with success, not only will it be easier to achieve our goals, but we will also enjoy the process and overcome obstacles with more confidence. The good news is that even though our beliefs and thoughts are deeply ingrained, we can reprogram our mind to think in a way that leads us to success.

The first thing we need to understand is that our mind works like a system. This system feeds on what we give it: our experiences, thoughts, emotions and beliefs. If we constantly feed our mind with negative thoughts, doubts or insecurities, that will be the programming it follows. However, if we begin to introduce positive thoughts, beliefs in our abilities and a clear vision of what we want to achieve, little by little our mind will adapt to this new pattern, making it part of its routine.

One of the most important aspects of reprogramming our minds for success is changing the way we think about ourselves. Often, the biggest obstacles we face are not external circumstances, but rather the barriers we put on ourselves. It's common to hear that inner voice telling us "I'm not good enough," "this is too hard," or "I'm not going to make it." These limiting thoughts are the result of negative programming, perhaps influenced by past experiences, criticism from others, or simply a fear of failure. The key is to identify these thoughts and replace them with positive, empowering affirmations.

For example, instead of thinking "this is too difficult for me," we can reprogram our mind to think "I can learn whatever it takes to overcome this challenge." This simple shift in thinking is more powerful than it seems. By replacing limiting thoughts with constructive and positive thoughts, we are telling our mind to trust in our abilities and that even if something is difficult, we are capable of facing it and moving forward. The mind, when repeatedly receiving these types of messages, will begin to operate under that premise and give us the confidence we need to move forward.

Another key aspect of programming our mind for success is setting clear goals. The human mind needs a purpose, a direction to move towards. When we don't have clear goals, it's easy to get lost in the daily routine or distracted by things that don't bring us closer to what we really want. However, when we define what we want, our mind automatically begins to focus on finding ways to achieve it. For example, if your goal is to improve at work or start a new project, it's important that this goal is clearly defined. Saying "I want to be successful" is not the same as saying "I want to learn a new skill in the next three months to improve my performance at work." The more specific our goals are, the easier it will be for our mind to find the way to achieve them.

An effective technique for reprogramming the mind is visualization. This is a simple but extremely powerful exercise. It involves clearly and vividly imagining the outcome we desire. Visualizing success in detail gives our mind a concrete image of what we want to achieve, which helps it work toward that goal. For example, if you want to be successful in an important presentation, you can visualize yourself giving the presentation with confidence, receiving praise from your peers, and feeling the satisfaction of having done a good job. This type of visualization not only increases our confidence, but it also gives our mind a positive reference to fall back on when fear or doubt tries to creep in.

Additionally, it is essential to practice consistency and discipline. Reprogramming your mind for success is not something that happens overnight. Just like any skill, it takes time and effort to change your thought patterns. At first, it may be a little difficult. Negative thoughts or old habits may try to creep back in, but this is where consistency plays a crucial role. Whenever you notice a negative or limiting thought, don't get frustrated. Instead, immediately replace it with a positive thought. Over time, this process will become more automatic and you will notice your mind responding more naturally with success-oriented thoughts.

It's equally important to surround yourself with influences that support this new programming. The people you interact with, the activities you do, and the content you consume have a huge impact on your mindset. If you surround yourself with people who believe in you, who support you, and who also have a success mindset, this reinforces your mind's new programming. Conversely, if you spend time with people who constantly doubt you or focus on the negative, it will be harder to maintain that positive mindset. So, part of programming your mind for success also involves creating an environment that pushes you to keep going.

Another fundamental tool in this process is gratitude. Gratitude is a practice that changes our perspective on life. When we focus on what we already have, instead of what we lack, we are training our mind to see opportunities instead of deficiencies. Gratitude helps us realize how far we have come, how much we have overcome, and what resources we already have. This type of thinking puts us in a state of abundance and predisposes us to attract more success into our lives. By practicing gratitude daily, we are not only reinforcing a positive mindset, but we are also creating an emotional environment that favors success.

Part of mental reprogramming also involves learning how to handle failure. Failure is an inevitable part of the road to success, and how we perceive it has a direct impact on whether we achieve our goals or not. Often times, when we fail at something, our mind tends to focus on the negative: "I didn't succeed," "I'm a failure," "I'm not capable of doing it." However, if we reprogram our mind to see failure as a learning opportunity, we'll be much more prepared to face future challenges. Instead of asking ourselves "why did I fail?" we can ask ourselves "what can I learn from this?" or "how can I do better next time?" This mindset shift transforms failure into a tool for growth and keeps us moving forward toward our goals.

The last key point to programming our mind for success is self-care. Often, in our quest for success, we forget the importance of taking care of ourselves. However, a healthy mind and body are essential to maintaining a positive and productive attitude. Sleeping well, eating a balanced diet, exercising regularly, and taking time to relax and unwind are practices that strengthen our mental capacity. When we feel good physically, our mind is more alert, more focused, and more capable of facing challenges with an optimistic attitude.

In short, programming your mind for success is a process that requires effort, discipline, and above all, consistency. By changing the way you think about yourself, aligning your goals, and using tools like visualization, gratitude, and positive handling of failure, you are creating a solid foundation for achieving your goals. In addition, surrounding yourself with positive influences and taking care of your physical and mental well-being reinforces this programming. Over time, you will notice how your mind adjusts to this new way of thinking, allowing you to move forward with more confidence, resilience, and determination towards the success you desire.

Spreading Positivity to Others

Spreading positivity to others is one of the best ways to impact the world around us. Our words, our actions, and the energy we project have great power. Often, we underestimate the impact we can have on the lives of others by simply being a source of positive energy. We've all had that experience of being around someone who, without saying much, makes us feel good, inspires us, or motivates us to see things in a different way. That's the magic of spreading positivity, and it's something we can all learn to do if we're aware of how our attitudes affect those around us.

The first step to transmitting positivity is to be aware of our own mental state. We cannot give what we do not have. If we are constantly in a state of negativity, pessimism or stress, it is difficult for our presence to be a positive influence on others. Therefore, the first work we must do is with ourselves. Cultivating a positive mindset not only benefits us, but also puts us in the position to be able to share that attitude with others. When we feel good, it is easier to transmit that good energy to those around us.

One of the simplest and most powerful ways to spread positivity is through our words. What we say has a direct impact on the people who listen to us. Words can be a tool to lift someone's spirits, give them confidence, or inspire someone to keep going. Small gestures, such as giving a genuine compliment, showing appreciation, or simply asking how someone is doing with genuine interest, can make a huge difference in a person's day. Sometimes, we don't realize how much good we can do by simply saying something kind. In a world where we often hear criticism, complaints, or negative comments, a little kindness and positivity can be a refreshing and necessary change.

Spreading positivity also involves learning to listen. We often think that being positive means always talking, encouraging, or sharing advice, but sometimes, the most positive thing we can do for someone is simply to be there and listen. When someone is going through a difficult time, what they need most is not always a solution, but to feel understood and supported. By listening attentively, without judging or interrupting, we are offering a safe space where the other person can express themselves and release their emotions. This act of active listening can be incredibly positive and can help the person see their problems from a clearer perspective.

In addition to what we say, our actions are also a powerful way to convey positivity. Our actions speak louder than our words. Being kind, helping others when they need it, showing empathy, and being willing to lend a helping hand are all effective ways to show that we really care about the people around us. Even small gestures, such as offering help without being asked or doing something for someone without expecting anything in return, can have a big impact. When we show with our actions that we are willing to contribute to the well-being of others, we are creating a positive environment where people feel valued and supported.

An important key to conveying positivity is being authentic. People can sense when someone is being fake or forcing a positive attitude. Genuine positivity isn't about ignoring problems or pretending everything is perfect. It's about acknowledging difficulties, but choosing to see the good in every situation and in every person. When we're authentic in our positivity, people around us notice and appreciate it. It's about finding that balance between being optimistic and being realistic, and showing that despite problems, there's always something worth smiling or fighting for.

It's important to understand that exuding positivity doesn't mean we have to be cheerful or motivated all the time. We all have difficult days, moments of stress or frustration, and that's completely normal. The key is how we handle those moments and how we impact others when things aren't going well. Even in the midst of difficulties, we can be a positive influence by showing resilience, patience, and a constructive attitude. When people see that, despite problems, we maintain a balanced and positive attitude, we are teaching them that it is possible to face challenges effectively without falling into pessimism.

It's also important to remember that spreading positivity doesn't always mean big gestures or words. Sometimes, just being a calm, kind presence in someone's life can make all the difference. We don't always need to solve other people's problems or be the source of great inspirations. Sometimes, just being there, showing support and understanding, is all someone needs to feel better. Our energy, our attitude, and how we respond to situations can influence how others feel, even without saying a word.

Another way to convey positivity is through our attitude toward mistakes and failures. We all make mistakes, and it's easy to fall into the trap of self-criticism or discouragement when things don't go our way. However, if we adopt a mindset that views mistakes as learning opportunities, we can share that perspective with others. Instead of punishing someone or making them feel bad about a mistake, we can offer support, help them see what they can learn from the situation, and motivate them to keep going. By showing that mistakes aren't the end of the world, we're teaching others to be kinder to themselves and to face challenges with a more positive attitude.

Finally, spreading positivity to others also involves taking care of ourselves. If we are not well, emotionally or physically, it will be difficult to be a source of support for others. Therefore, it is important to pay attention to our own needs and make sure that we are in a good place mentally and emotionally. Practicing self-care is not a selfish act, but a way to ensure that we are in a position to offer our best to others. Whether it is taking time to relax, practicing our own stress management techniques, or seeking help when we need it, taking care of our mental and physical health allows us to be more present and a positive influence for those around us.

In conclusion, spreading positivity to others is a skill we can all develop. It's about being aware of our words, our actions, and our attitude, and understanding the impact we have on the lives of those around us. From offering a kind word to listening attentively, through our helpful gestures to the way we face challenges, each of our interactions is an opportunity to make the world a little more positive. And the best part is that by doing this, we are not only improving the lives of others, but our own as well.

How to Turn Failure into Success

Failure is something we all experience at some point in our lives. Often, we see it as a negative thing, as an obstacle that stands in our way to success. However, what many people don't realize is that failure can be one of the greatest teachers we have. Turning failure into success is not only possible, but it's a key skill for anyone who wants to achieve their goals and grow throughout their life. What's important is not how many times we fail, but how we respond to those failures and what we learn from them.

One of the first things we need to understand is that failure is not the opposite of success. Many people think that if they fail, it means they don't have what it takes to succeed. But in reality, failure is part of the path to success. Every time we fail, we learn something new about ourselves, our abilities, and what we're trying to accomplish. These learnings are like pieces of a puzzle that, little by little, bring us closer to success. If we never failed, we'd never know what adjustments we needed to make or what skills we needed to improve.

One of the keys to turning failure into success is changing our mindset about what it means to fail. Instead of seeing failure as a bad thing, we can start seeing it as an opportunity for growth. Every time something doesn't go the way we expected, we have the opportunity to reflect on what happened and ask ourselves, "What can I learn from this?" This question is critical, because it helps us focus on the lessons that failure is teaching us. Maybe we discover that we need more practice at a certain skill, or that the strategy we were using wasn't the right one. Whatever the lesson, learning from our mistakes makes us stronger and more capable of facing future challenges.

It is important to understand that many of the most successful people in the world have experienced failures along the way. In fact, some of the greatest achievements in history have been the result of repeated failures. A classic example is Thomas Edison, who failed thousands of times before inventing the light bulb. When asked about his failures, he replied that he had not failed, but that he had found thousands of ways in which it did not work. This type of mindset is crucial. Edison did not see his failures as the end of the road, but rather as an inevitable part of the process of discovery. Each failed attempt brought him closer to his goal, because he learned something new with each mistake.

Another important aspect of turning failure into success is not being afraid to fail. Often, the fear of failure paralyzes us and prevents us from taking risks or trying new things. But what we often forget is that without risk, there is no reward. If we always play it safe, we will never know what we are truly capable of. Failure is part of any meaningful endeavor, and accepting this frees us from the pressure of having to get everything right the first time. The more times we dare to fail, the more opportunities we have to learn, improve, and ultimately achieve success.

It's also helpful to surround yourself with people who understand the value of failure and who support you through your tough times. Sometimes when you fail, you feel alone or ashamed, like you're the only one struggling. But the reality is that everyone, at some point, has faced failure. Having a support group, whether it's friends, family, or mentors, can help you maintain a positive outlook and not give up. These people can remind you that failure isn't the end, but just part of the process.

It's also important not to let failure define our self-esteem. Many people feel that when they fail, it means they're not good enough or capable enough. But it's crucial to remember that failure doesn't define who we are. One mistake or setback doesn't make us any less valuable as people. What really matters is how we react to failure and what we do with what we've learned. If we let failure get us down, we're missing out on a huge opportunity for growth. Instead, if we use it as a platform to propel us forward, we'll be much closer to achieving our goals.

Another strategy for turning failure into success is persistence. Sometimes, after a failure, the temptation to give up can be very strong. It may seem easier to abandon the goal than to keep going after a fall. But the difference between those who achieve success and those who don't is often the ability to keep trying, even when things don't go as expected. Persistence is key. Each failed attempt brings us a little closer to our goal, as long as we don't stop trying. History is full of examples of people who failed again and again, but who eventually achieved success because they never stopped pursuing their dreams.

To turn failure into success, it's also important to be flexible. Sometimes failure shows us that we need to change direction or adjust our strategies. Being able to adapt to circumstances and make changes when necessary is a key skill on the path to success. If we stubbornly cling to one way of doing things, we're likely to find ourselves failing again and again. But if we're willing to be flexible and try new approaches, we increase our chances of finding a solution that works.

Finally, it's crucial to maintain a positive attitude toward failure. Although it can be frustrating or painful to fail, it's important not to lose sight of the fact that every setback provides us with an opportunity to learn and improve. Maintaining an optimistic outlook helps us not get discouraged and keep moving forward. Let's remember that failure is not permanent. It's just a step on the road to success, and if we face it with an open and positive mindset, we can transform even the most difficult moments into opportunities for growth and achievement.

In short, turning failure into success is all about mindset and approach. It's about seeing failures not as insurmountable obstacles, but as opportunities to learn, grow, and improve. By changing our perspective on failure, learning from our mistakes, staying persistent, and being flexible in our approach, we can transform any setback into a stepping stone to success. So the next time you face failure, remember that you're one step closer to achieving what you set out to do.

Positive Thinking in Stress Management

Stress is an unavoidable part of life. We've all felt that pressure in our chest, that anxiety that seems to paralyze us, or that feeling of being overwhelmed by circumstances at some point. Whether it's work, school, family problems, or any other situation, stress can creep up and affect us in different ways. What many people don't know, however, is that positive thinking can be a very powerful tool for managing and reducing stress. Instead of letting stress get the better of us, we can learn to manage it effectively by changing the way we think about the situations that cause it.

Positive thinking isn't about ignoring problems or pretending that everything is okay when it clearly isn't. Rather, it's about changing our perspective on what's happening. When faced with a stressful situation, often our first reaction is to panic or think of the worst that could happen. This, of course, only makes the problem worse, as we focus on the negative and get carried away by fear and anxiety. Positive thinking, on the other hand, invites us to stop for a moment, breathe, and reframe the situation from a more constructive point of view.

One way to begin applying positive thinking to stress management is to learn to identify the automatic negative thoughts that come to mind during times of stress. These thoughts are often quick and almost automatic, and are often along the lines of, "I can't handle this," "This is too much for me," or "Everything is going to go wrong." These thoughts increase our stress level and make us feel powerless in the face of problems. The key is to stop, acknowledge these thoughts, and challenge them. Instead of assuming the worst, we can ask ourselves, "Is it really as bad as it seems?" or "What can I do to fix this?"

Simply pausing and questioning our negative thoughts puts us in a more powerful position in the face of stress. Often, we realize that the situation is not as dire as we initially thought, or that we have more control over it than we had believed. This doesn't mean that the problem goes away, but at least it helps us see it in a more manageable way. Replacing our negative thoughts with more positive or realistic thoughts gives us a greater sense of control and reduces anxiety.

Another very useful technique in stress management through positive thinking is the practice of gratitude. When we are stressed, we tend to focus only on what is wrong in our lives. We forget about the good things, no matter how small, and this further amplifies our feeling of being overwhelmed. Taking a few minutes to reflect on the things we are grateful for can completely change our perspective. It can be something as simple as being grateful for being healthy, having a roof over our head, or the support of a loved one. This small shift in focus can significantly reduce stress as it reminds us that despite the problems, there are also many good things in our lives.

Positive thinking also helps us manage stress by fostering a solution mindset rather than a problem mindset. When we're stressed, it's easy to get stuck in a cycle of worry, mulling over the problem without looking for a way out. This only increases our stress level. But when we shift our focus to the solution, we start thinking about what we can do to improve the situation. No matter how small the step, the fact that we're taking action makes us feel more in control and less overwhelmed. The simple act of shifting from worry to action already reduces stress considerably.

A key aspect of positive thinking is that it helps us stay calm during times of stress. Stress tends to trigger our "fight or flight" response, a natural reaction of the body to situations perceived as threatening. This response prepares us to face danger, but in everyday situations, such as a problem at work or an argument with someone, this reaction can backfire. It puts us in a constant state of alert and increases our anxiety. Positive thinking allows us to stop, breathe, and respond more calmly and rationally. Instead of reacting impulsively, we can take a moment to think about how best to handle the situation.

Plus, positive thinking helps us see stress from a different perspective. Instead of seeing stress as something entirely negative, we can start to see it as an opportunity for growth. Every challenge we face gives us a chance to learn something new about ourselves and develop new skills. For example, if we're stressed out by an overwhelming workload, maybe it's an opportunity to learn how to manage our time better or to delegate tasks. If we see stress as an opportunity instead of a threat, it completely changes the way we experience it.

It's important to note that positive thinking doesn't eliminate stress completely. We will all face difficult situations at some point, and there will be times when stress is unavoidable. What positive thinking does do, however, is reduce the impact that stress has on us. It allows us to handle situations better and helps us prevent stress from building up to the point where it affects our health or relationships.

Another technique that goes hand in hand with positive thinking in stress management is self-care. Stress can drain us physically and mentally, and if we don't take care of ourselves, it's harder to maintain a positive attitude. Making time to relax, exercising, eating well, and getting enough sleep are all key aspects of staying balanced. When we feel good physically, it's easier to think positively and deal with stress with a clearer mind. Taking care of ourselves isn't a luxury, it's a necessity, especially when we're dealing with stressful situations.

It is also helpful to practice deep breathing or meditation as ways to calm the mind and reduce stress. These techniques help us focus on the present and let go of negative thoughts or worries that keep us stressed. Taking a few minutes a day to breathe deeply or meditate can make a big difference in how we handle stress throughout the day. It allows us to unwind, relax and recharge, which in turn helps us maintain a positive attitude.

In conclusion, positive thinking is a powerful tool for managing stress. By shifting our perspective, challenging negative thoughts, focusing on solutions, and practicing gratitude, we can reduce the impact of stress on our lives. We can't avoid stress altogether, but we can choose how we respond to it. And by choosing positive thinking, we're not only managing stress better, but we're also creating a healthier, more balanced mental environment for ourselves. With practice and dedication, we can learn to face life's stressful situations with a calmer, more positive attitude.

The Mindset of a Winner

A winner's mindset isn't something you're born with, it's something you develop over time. Often times, we associate the word "winner" with someone who is successful at what they do, someone who always achieves what they set out to do. But what really defines a winner isn't just the result, but how they think, how they face challenges, and how they persevere, even when things aren't going well. Having a winner's mindset doesn't mean always winning, but rather learning to keep going despite the failures, difficulties, and obstacles that come your way.

The key to a winner's mindset is their focus on growth. For someone with this mindset, every situation, whether a success or a failure, is an opportunity to learn and improve. A winner isn't satisfied with what they already know or what they've already accomplished, but is always looking for ways to grow and develop. They don't see challenges as insurmountable barriers, but rather as opportunities to develop new skills or discover creative ways to overcome problems. This growth mindset is what allows winners to keep moving forward, even when they face difficulties.

Another important aspect of a winner's mindset is self-belief. This doesn't mean having blind confidence or thinking you're perfect, but rather trusting in your ability to improve and overcome challenges. A winner believes that with effort and dedication, they can achieve what they set out to do, even if it seems difficult or impossible at first. This self-confidence is what allows them to take risks, step out of their comfort zone, and not fear failure. They know that failure is part of the process and that each failed attempt brings them one step closer to their goal.

Perseverance is another essential trait in a winner's mindset. People with this mindset don't give up easily. They understand that success doesn't always come right away and that in many cases, it will require consistent effort over time. Winners aren't discouraged by setbacks or hardships. Instead of seeing them as signs that they should give up, they see them as tests that will make them stronger and more capable in the future.

Perseverance is what allows them to keep going when others stop. No matter how many times they fail, they are always willing to try one more time.

Additionally, a winner has a solution-oriented mindset. Instead of focusing on problems or difficulties, they actively look for ways to solve them. This doesn't mean they ignore problems, but rather that they don't get stuck on them. A winner constantly asks themselves, "What can I do to improve this situation?" or "How can I overcome this obstacle?" By focusing on solutions rather than problems, they maintain a positive and proactive attitude, which allows them to move forward, even in the most difficult circumstances.

Another important characteristic of a winner's mindset is resilience. Life is full of ups and downs, and a winner understands that tough times are temporary. Resilience is the ability to bounce back quickly from hardship, adapt to change, and keep moving forward even when things don't go as expected. Winners don't sit around ruing what went wrong, but rather learn from their mistakes and use those lessons to improve. They know that every failure is an opportunity to grow and that the true measure of success is not how many times you fall, but how many times you get back up.

A winner's mindset is also characterized by their ability to stay focused on their goals. It's easy to get distracted by difficulties or criticism, but a winner knows how to keep their attention on what really matters. They have a clear vision of what they want to accomplish and don't let distractions or obstacles steer them off course. This doesn't mean they're rigid in their approach; in fact, winners are flexible and willing to adjust their plan when necessary. But they never lose sight of their end goal. This ability to stay focused is what allows them to move forward, even when others lose direction.

Additionally, winners don't see success as an individual thing. They understand that true success often requires collaboration and support from others. They aren't afraid to ask for help when they need it and value teamwork. They know that surrounding themselves with positive, success-minded people can make a huge difference in their achievements. A winner knows that the people they associate with can influence their mindset, so they consciously choose to be around people who inspire them, motivate them, and push them to be better.

Another critical aspect of a winner's mindset is self-discipline. To achieve success in any area of life, you need to have the ability to work consistently, even when you don't feel motivated or when circumstances aren't ideal. Winners know that motivation is fleeting, but self-discipline is what will keep them on track toward their long-term goals. They don't rely solely on feeling inspired or motivated. Instead, they have developed habits that keep them moving, even when things get tough. Self-discipline is what allows them to overcome procrastination, stay focused, and continue working toward their goals, day after day.

It's also important to mention that a winner's mindset includes a strong work ethic. Winners aren't afraid to put in the effort necessary to achieve their goals. They know that success doesn't come by accident or luck, but rather as a result of hard, consistent work. They have an attitude of "if I want something, I have to work for it." And while that work can sometimes be arduous and difficult, they see it as an essential part of the process. This work ethic allows them to face any challenge with the confidence that, with the right amount of effort, they can overcome it.

Finally, a winner's mindset is based on the belief that there is always room for improvement. No matter how successful someone is, a true winner never stops learning. They are constantly looking for ways to improve, whether it's by acquiring new skills, learning from their mistakes, or seeking feedback from others. They know that the road to success doesn't have a fixed end, but rather is a continuous journey of personal growth and improvement. This mindset of constant learning allows them to stay competitive and always one step ahead.

In short, a winner's mindset is not just about winning in the traditional sense of the word. It is about adopting a growth mindset, learning from mistakes, staying focused on solutions, being resilient in the face of challenges, and working with self-discipline and determination toward goals. Having a winner's mindset means believing in yourself, but also being willing to work hard, constantly learn, and never give up, no matter how many times things don't go the way we expected. This is the true essence of what it means to be a winner.

Building Positive Habits

Building positive habits is one of the most important keys to living a full and satisfying life. Often, when we think about habits, we only focus on the actions we repeat day after day, such as brushing our teeth or having a cup of coffee in the morning. But habits are much more than just routines; they are the repeated actions that form the foundation of our lives. If we want to improve our mental, physical, and emotional health, we need to start by building habits that help us achieve those goals. The good news is that positive habits are not something out of reach. Anyone can develop them, but, like everything valuable in life, it requires time, patience, and constant effort.

To understand how to build positive habits, we first need to know what a habit is. A habit is an action that we repeat automatically, without having to think much about it. At first, when we start doing something new, we have to be very conscious of what we are doing, but with time and repetition, that action becomes part of our daily routine. For example, when we start learning to drive a car, every little movement requires our attention. But after a while, driving becomes second nature, almost automatic. That's how habits work. The more we repeat an action, the easier and more natural it becomes.

The first step to building positive habits is to identify which areas of our life we want to improve. This could be our health, our relationships, our work, or even our mental attitude. Often, small changes can lead to big results over time. For example, if we want to improve our physical health, a positive habit might be going for a 10-minute walk every day. If we want to improve our relationships, a positive habit could be taking a few minutes each day to text a friend or family member, just to show them that we care. If we want to improve our mental health, we could start practicing gratitude, taking a few minutes each day to reflect on the good things we have in our life.

It's important to start with small, achievable habits. Many people fail at creating positive habits because they try to make changes that are too big or too fast. For example, if we've never exercised before and suddenly decide that we're going to do an hour of intense exercise every day, we're likely to get discouraged and give up the habit after just a few days. On the other hand, if we start with something small, like walking for 10 minutes a day, we're much more likely to stick with it long-term. Over time, we can gradually increase the duration or intensity, but the most important thing is to start in a realistic and sustainable way.

Consistency is another key factor in building positive habits. For a habit to really become ingrained in our daily routine, we need to do it consistently, ideally every day. Repetition is what turns an action into a habit. The more we repeat an action, the easier it becomes. At first, it may feel a little difficult or awkward, but over time, it becomes a natural part of our life. It's like learning to ride a bike. At first, we may need help or support, but with consistent practice, we'll eventually be able to do it effortlessly.

Another important aspect is to be patient. Habits don't form overnight. According to some studies, it can take anywhere from 21 to 66 days, or even longer, for a new habit to become part of our daily routine. This means that it's completely normal to struggle at first. There will be days when we don't feel like taking that daily walk, or when we forget to practice gratitude. But the important thing is to not give up. One bad day doesn't mean all progress is lost. If we fail one day, we simply try again the next day. It's long-term consistency that matters, not perfection.

A useful trick to make it easier to create positive habits is to link the new habit we want to develop to something we already do regularly. This is known as "habit stacking." For example, if we want to create a habit of meditating every day, we could do it right after we brush our teeth in the morning, since brushing our teeth is something we already do automatically. This way, it's easier to integrate the new habit into our daily routine. Another example would be listening to an educational podcast while driving to work or drinking a glass of water right after we wake up. By linking a new habit to an existing one, we're much more likely to stick with it.

Motivation is another key piece in building positive habits. We need to be clear about why we are making that change and how it will benefit us in the long run. For example, if our goal is to exercise regularly, the motivation might be to improve our health, increase our energy, or feel better about ourselves. If we are clear about the "why" behind the habit, it will be easier to stick with it, even when we don't feel like it. It's helpful to remember that the benefits of positive habits are often not seen right away. We may not notice big changes at first, but over time, those small daily efforts add up and produce significant results.

An interesting aspect of habits is that they often have a domino effect on other areas of our lives. This means that by developing a positive habit in one area, it is likely to start positively influencing others. For example, if we start exercising regularly, we may also start eating healthier or sleeping better. Similarly, if we develop the habit of gratitude, we may start feeling more optimistic and having better relationships with others. Positive habits tend to reinforce each other, creating a virtuous cycle in our lives.

Of course, building positive habits isn't just a matter of eliminating bad habits. Sometimes, bad habits can interfere with the new habits we want to develop. For example, if we want to read more, but we have a habit of spending hours in front of the TV or social media, it will be difficult to find time for reading. In these cases, it's important to be aware of the negative habits that are holding us back and work on replacing them with more constructive habits. Rather than trying to eliminate a bad habit cold turkey, it can be helpful to replace it with something positive. For example, if we want to stop constantly checking our phone, we could replace that habit with reading a book or doing a productive activity.

In short, building positive habits is one of the best ways to improve our lives sustainably. By identifying the areas we want to improve, starting with small changes, being consistent and patient, and finding ways to integrate the new habits into our daily routine, we can develop habits that help us live a fuller, healthier, and more satisfying life. Habits are not something that is formed overnight, but with effort and dedication, anyone can develop positive habits that allow them to achieve their goals and improve their well-being in the long term.

The Power of Affirmations

The power of affirmations is an incredibly valuable tool that can transform the way we think and feel about ourselves and the world around us. Affirmations are positive statements that we repeat, with the intention of influencing our thoughts and, eventually, our actions. Although at first glance it may seem like a very simple technique, the impact it can have on our lives is profound. By repeating positive affirmations, we are slowly reprogramming our mind to focus on the positive, on what we can achieve, and on opportunities instead of obstacles. It is a way of training our mind to align with our goals and dreams.

The principle behind affirmations is that our thoughts have a great deal of power over how we experience life. We all have an inner voice that talks to us throughout the day, a sort of self-talk that can be positive or negative. If we are constantly thinking about what we can't do, our mistakes, or what we lack, those negative thoughts can influence the way we act and see the world. On the other hand, if we choose to replace those negative thoughts with positive affirmations, we are creating a new reality for ourselves, one in which we believe more in our capabilities and our worth.

One of the most important aspects of affirmations is that they help change the way we perceive our capabilities. Often, we limit ourselves because we believe that we are not good enough, smart enough, or strong enough to achieve something. These limiting beliefs hold us back before we even try. But by using affirmations like "I am capable of achieving anything I set my mind to" or "I have the power to change my life for the better," we begin to change those negative beliefs and replace them with empowering beliefs. When we repeat these affirmations with conviction and frequently, we begin to truly believe them, and this is reflected in the way we act.

It's important to note that affirmations don't work magically or instantly. It's not just about repeating empty words and expecting everything to change overnight. Affirmations are a tool that helps us train our mind, and like any training, it takes time and practice. At first, we may not fully believe in the affirmations we're saying, especially if they're far removed from our current reality. For example, if we say "I have a life full of success and happiness" when we're going through a difficult time, our mind might resist accepting that affirmation. But the more we repeat it, the more we begin to internalize that message, and little by little our perspective begins to change.

Another important benefit of affirmations is that they help us develop greater self-confidence. When we repeat phrases like "I am valuable" or "I am confident in my abilities," we are reinforcing our self-esteem. Over time, this self-confidence begins to manifest itself in our actions. We dare to take more risks, to step out of our comfort zone, and to pursue our dreams with greater determination. Self-confidence doesn't just come out of nowhere, it's something that is built over time, and affirmations are a great way to start cementing it. By strengthening our inner confidence, we also become more resilient in the face of challenges that may arise along the way.

Affirmations also help us focus on what we want instead of what we don't want. Often, our worries and fears take up much of our attention. We worry about what could go wrong, what mistakes we might make, or what difficulties we might face. Without realizing it, these negative thoughts consume us and prevent us from moving forward. Affirmations help us redirect our attention toward the positive, toward our goals and desires. Instead of focusing on what we fear, we focus on what we want to attract into our lives. This shift in focus is critical, as what we think tends to manifest in our actions and results.

An interesting aspect of affirmations is that they can also influence our physical health. Several studies have shown that our thoughts and emotions have a direct impact on our physical well-being. When we fill ourselves with negative thoughts, our body reacts with stress, which can affect our immune system, our digestion, and our ability to rest well. Conversely, when we practice positive affirmations, we reduce stress and improve our overall health. This is because affirmations help us maintain a more relaxed and optimistic mental attitude, allowing our body to function more efficiently.

It is important that affirmations are stated clearly and in the present tense. Instead of saying, "I will be successful someday," it is much more effective to say, "I am successful." The reason for this is that our mind responds better to affirmations that are stated as if they are already a reality. When we say, "I will be...", we are projecting that goal into an uncertain future, which makes our mind see it as something far away and difficult to achieve. By saying, "I am successful," we are affirming that we are already on the path to success, and our mind begins to work accordingly. We move toward that affirmation because we already feel connected to it.

Another tip for making affirmations effective is to combine them with emotions. When we repeat an affirmation, it is important to feel it, to truly believe it. Emotions are a powerful part of the human mind, and when we combine words with emotions, those words have a much greater impact. For example, if we say "I am happy," we should try to connect with the feeling of happiness. Let us recall a time when we felt really happy and try to relive that emotion while repeating the affirmation. By doing this, we are reinforcing the message in our mind in a much deeper way.

Furthermore, affirmations not only serve to improve our personal lives, but they also have an impact on our relationships with others. When we begin to believe in our own worth and capabilities, we also improve the way we interact with the people around us. We become more self-confident, which allows us to form healthier and more authentic relationships. We can also use affirmations to improve our relationships, saying things like, "I attract positive people into my life," or "My relationships are full of love and understanding." These affirmations help create a mental environment that fosters positive interactions.

For affirmations to really work, it's essential to incorporate them into our daily routine. They can be part of our morning ritual, repeating them as we prepare for the day, or they can be something we practice before bed to end the day on a positive note. Some people also find it helpful to write down their affirmations in a notebook or on sticky notes that they place in visible places, such as the bathroom mirror or work desk. This way, we're constantly reminding ourselves of the positive messages we want to instill in our minds.

In short, the power of affirmations lies in their ability to transform the way we think and, in the long run, the way we live. Although they may seem simple, affirmations have a profound impact on our self-confidence, the way we face challenges, and the way we relate to the world. They are a powerful tool to reprogram our mind, moving us away from negative thoughts and towards a more positive, fulfilling, and successful life. Like any tool, it requires practice and consistency, but the results are worth it. Affirmations allow us to be the creators of our reality, guiding our mind towards what we truly wish to achieve in life.

Alexa Murphy

The Role of Self-Esteem in Positive Psychology

Self-esteem is one of the fundamental pillars in positive psychology, and it plays a crucial role in how we approach life, make decisions, and relate to others. Self-esteem, in simple terms, is the value we give ourselves, the perception we have of our worth and our capabilities. It is the judgment we make about who we are and how we compare to the rest of the world. When we have high self-esteem, we feel confident, capable, and worthy of love and respect. When our self-esteem is low, we tend to doubt ourselves, feel insecure, and believe that we do not deserve the best.

Positive psychology, which focuses on well-being and how we can cultivate a more fulfilling and satisfying life, recognizes that self-esteem is an essential component of achieving well-being. If we don't believe in ourselves, it's difficult to develop a positive mindset toward life. Self-esteem acts as a solid foundation upon which to build an optimistic attitude and a fulfilling life. When a person feels good about themselves, they become more resilient to difficulties, more open to new experiences, and more willing to take risks to achieve their goals.

One of the most important aspects of self-esteem is that it directly affects our perception of the world. When we have good self-esteem, we tend to see the world in a more positive light. Difficulties don't seem so insurmountable, criticism doesn't hurt as much, and failures are seen as opportunities to learn. On the other hand, when our self-esteem is low, the world can seem like a hostile place full of obstacles. Everything feels more complicated, and mistakes are seen as evidence of our supposed inability. Self-esteem, in that sense, acts as a filter through which we interpret reality. If the filter is positive, our life experience will be more pleasant and bearable. If the filter is negative, we will feel more frustrated and unmotivated.

An important point to consider is that self-esteem is not something fixed or immutable. It can improve or deteriorate depending on how we treat ourselves and the experiences we go through. The good news is that we can all work on improving our self-esteem, no matter where we are. The key is to develop a kinder and more compassionate relationship with ourselves. Instead of constantly criticizing ourselves for our mistakes or negatively comparing ourselves to others, we must learn to recognize our intrinsic value. We all make mistakes, we all have moments of weakness, but that does not define our worth. Self-esteem is strengthened when we accept that we are human, imperfect, and still deserving of respect and love.

The first step to improving self-esteem is practicing self-acceptance. This means accepting who we are, with our strengths and weaknesses, without trying to change ourselves or judging ourselves harshly. Self-acceptance doesn't mean settling or stopping improving, but rather it involves understanding that our worth isn't dependent on our actions or accomplishments. We are valuable simply for being who we are. This is a central concept in positive psychology—the idea that we all have intrinsic value that isn't dependent on external factors. Often, our self-esteem suffers because we base our worth on accomplishments, the opinions of others, or comparisons to other people. But when we realize that our worth is independent of those things, we can begin to feel more confident and at peace with ourselves.

Another key aspect of self-esteem is self-compassion. We are often our own harshest critics. We say things to ourselves that we would never say to another person, and we are quick to judge ourselves when we make a mistake. Self-compassion invites us to treat ourselves with the same kindness and understanding that we would show a friend. Instead of beating ourselves up for our shortcomings, we can learn to be more understanding of ourselves. We all make mistakes, we all have bad days, but that doesn't mean we're worthless. Practicing self-compassion helps us be kinder to ourselves, which in turn strengthens our self-esteem.

Furthermore, it is important to recognize that self-esteem is also related to how we take care of ourselves. When we value ourselves, we treat ourselves with respect and attention. This is reflected in our daily actions, from the way we take care of our physical health to how we manage our emotions and relationships. Taking care of ourselves is a way of telling ourselves that we are important, that we deserve time, effort, and dedication. If we constantly neglect ourselves or put ourselves last, our self-esteem suffers. But when we make a conscious effort to take care of ourselves, we send a powerful message to our mind: "I am worthy of being cared for."

An effective strategy for improving self-esteem is to focus on our strengths. Often, we tend to focus on our weaknesses, what we lack, or what we think we don't do well. This negative focus can erode our self-esteem over time. Instead, it's helpful to make a list of our positive qualities, talents, and accomplishments. We all have strengths, even if we sometimes don't recognize them. By focusing on what we do well, rather than what we think we do poorly, we begin to change the internal narrative and cultivate healthier self-esteem.

It's important to note that self-esteem isn't about being arrogant or thinking you're better than others. Healthy self-esteem is based on a sense of self-worth that doesn't require comparison. When we truly value ourselves, we don't feel the need to put others down or constantly compete. In fact, people with strong self-esteem tend to be more generous and understanding toward others, because they don't feel like their worth is at stake. They can celebrate others' successes without feeling envious, and they can handle criticism without breaking down, because their sense of worth comes from within.

Self-esteem also influences how we relate to the world and the people around us. When we have good self-esteem, we set healthier boundaries, we know what we deserve, and we don't accept less than what we're worth. This is reflected in our personal, work, and social relationships. People with high self-esteem tend to surround themselves with more balanced and respectful relationships, as they don't seek external validation or allow others to treat them poorly. In contrast, low self-esteem can lead us to accept toxic behaviors or constantly seek approval from others, which can negatively affect our quality of life.

In short, self-esteem plays an essential role in positive psychology because it is the foundation of how we feel about ourselves and the world. By developing healthy self-esteem, we become more resilient, more optimistic, and better able to face life's challenges. Improving our self-esteem is a process that takes time and effort, but the benefits are immense. When we truly value ourselves, we can live a fuller, more authentic, and more positive life. The key is self-acceptance, self-compassion, and the recognition of our strengths, understanding that we are all worthy of love, respect, and happiness.

Living a Full Life with Positive Psychology

Living a full life is one of the greatest desires we have as human beings. We all want to feel happy, fulfilled and at peace with ourselves and with others. However, we often find ourselves trapped in worries, in situations that do not make us feel good or in thoughts that limit us. This is where positive psychology comes into play, offering us tools and approaches to create a more satisfying life, focusing on what makes us feel good, instead of getting caught up in the negative aspects of life.

Positive psychology teaches us that a full life is not one that is free of problems or difficulties, because that is impossible. We all, at some point, face obstacles, disappointments or moments of sadness. But what we can control is the way we respond to those situations. A full life, then, is not the absence of problems, but the ability to face them in a positive way, with the confidence that there is always a way out, a solution or a lesson behind every challenge.

One of the fundamental pillars of living a full life is learning to focus on the positive. This doesn't mean ignoring the negative or pretending that problems don't exist, but rather changing our focus. For example, instead of concentrating on what we lack, what we haven't achieved, or what has gone wrong, we can focus on what we do have, on our achievements, and on the things that have gone well. This simple change in perspective can have a huge impact on how we feel and how we face each day.

Gratitude is another powerful tool for living a full life. When we practice gratitude on a regular basis, we begin to notice the good things around us, no matter how small. Maybe it was a nice conversation with a friend, a delicious meal, or even just enjoying a quiet moment. These small positive experiences, when consciously appreciated, begin to add up, and over time make us feel more satisfied and happy with our lives. It's not about living in anticipation of big events or accomplishments to feel good, but about recognizing that every day has something to offer, something to be grateful for.

Another key aspect of a fulfilling life is taking care of our relationships. Humans are social by nature, and our connections with others play a crucial role in our happiness. Positive, healthy relationships provide us with emotional support, motivate us, and make us feel part of something bigger. In positive psychology, there is a lot of talk about the importance of surrounding ourselves with people who push us to be our best selves, who encourage us, and who accompany us through difficult times. Maintaining healthy, nurturing relationships is essential for our long-term well-being.

Aside from our relationships with others, the relationship we have with ourselves is also crucial. We can often be our own worst critics. We judge ourselves harshly, punish ourselves for our mistakes, and treat ourselves in ways we would never treat someone else. To live a full life, it is important to cultivate self-compassion and self-respect. We must learn to be kind to ourselves, accept ourselves as we are, and allow ourselves to fail without feeling less for it. A full life is not about perfection, but about accepting our humanity and moving forward with self-love, without punishing ourselves for our flaws.

Another essential tool that positive psychology offers us is the development of personal strengths. Each of us has talents, skills, or characteristics that make us unique. Identifying and leveraging those strengths can be a great step toward a more fulfilling life. For example, if you are someone who is naturally curious, you can seek out activities or jobs that stimulate that curiosity. If you have a strong ability to listen and empathize, you can focus on relationships or jobs that require those skills. When we align our daily actions with our strengths, we not only feel more fulfilled, but we also experience a greater sense of purpose and satisfaction.

A sense of purpose is undoubtedly a key element to living a full life. Knowing that our actions have meaning and that what we do matters fills us with energy and motivation. It's not just about having a job or a long-term goal, but about finding purpose in the little things. It can be from the care we give to our relationships, to the impact we want to have on our community or the world. Living with purpose helps us overcome difficult times and drives us to move forward with hope and determination.

In addition to purpose, balance is also important. Sometimes, in our quest for success or fulfillment, we can forget the importance of having balance in our lives. Work is important, but so is rest, time for ourselves, and enjoying the little things. A full life includes moments of effort and dedication, but also moments of relaxation, fun, and disconnection. Finding this balance is key to maintaining a healthy and happy life over time.

One aspect that we often overlook, but which is essential to living a full life, is taking care of our physical and mental health. We cannot have a satisfying life if we neglect our body or our mind. Regular exercise, a balanced diet, adequate rest and taking care of our emotions are essential pieces of the well-being puzzle. Positive psychology reminds us that well-being is a comprehensive state that includes both the physical and mental. By taking care of our body, we are also taking care of our mind and vice versa.

Finally, living a full life with positive psychology involves having a growth mindset. This means being open to learning, changing, and constantly improving. Life will always be full of challenges and situations that will take us out of our comfort zone, but if we adopt a growth mindset, we can see those moments as opportunities to learn and evolve. It's not about avoiding problems or having all the answers, but about being willing to face each challenge with the confidence that we can come out stronger on the other side.

In short, living a full life with positive psychology is about focusing our mind on what makes us feel good, cultivating gratitude, caring for our relationships, respecting ourselves, developing our strengths, finding purpose, maintaining balance, and taking care of our physical and mental health. It is a continuous path of growth and self-discovery, in which we learn to see life with optimism, without denying difficulties, but facing them with a positive attitude. At the end of the day, fulfillment is not in what we have or achieve, but in how we choose to live, how we treat ourselves and others, and how we face each moment, big or small, with an open and positive mindset.